Oprah Winfrey

Black History Biographies

Izzi Howell

CRABTREE
PUBLISHING COMPANY
WWW.CRABTREEBOOKS.COM

CRABTREE PUBLISHING COMPANY
WWW.CRABTREEBOOKS.COM

Published in Canada
Crabtree Publishing
616 Welland Ave.
St. Catharines, Ontario
L2M 5V6

Published in the United States
Crabtree Publishing
347 Fifth Avenue
Suite 1402–145
New York, NY 10016

*All words in **bold** appear in the glossary on page 23.*

Published in 2021 by Crabtree Publishing Company

All rights reserved. No part of this publication may be reproduced, stored in a retrieval system or be transmitted in any form or by any means, electronic, mechanical, photocopying, recording, or otherwise, without the prior written permission of the copyright owner.

First published by The Watts Publishing Group
Copyright © The Watts Publishing Group, 2019

Author: Izzi Howell
Editorial director: Kathy Middleton
Series editor: Izzi Howell
Editor: Ellen Rodger
Series designer: Rocket Design Ltd
Designer: Clare Nicholas
Proofreader: Crystal Sikkens
Production coordinator and Prepress technician: Ken Wright
Print coordinator: Katherine Berti
Literacy consultant: Kate Ruttle

The publisher would like to thank the following for permission to reproduce their pictures: Alamy: Jensen Sutta cover, Everett Collection 7, King World Productions/courtesy Everett Collection 10, NBC/Courtesy: Everett Collection 11, PictureLux/The Hollywood Archive 12, Patti McConville 14, Africa Media Online 16; Getty: Mark Sagliocco/FilmMagic 4, Robert Abbott Sengstacke 6t, young84 6b, Afro American Newspapers/Gado 9, George Pimentel/WireImage 13, Alberto E. Rodriguez 15b, Michelly Rall/WireImage 17, MANDEL NGAN/AFP 20, Michael Kovac/Getty Images for Moet & Chandon 21; Shutterstock: Krista Kennell title page, Everett Collection 15 and 18, Serggod 8, BortN66 9, Keith Homan 15t, Ink Drop 19.

Every attempt has been made to clear copyright. Should there be any inadvertent omission please apply to the publisher for rectification.

Printed in the U.S.A./122020/CG20201014

Library and Achives Canada Cataloguing in Publication

Title: Oprah Winfrey / Izzi Howell.
Names: Howell, Izzi, author.
Description: Series statement: Black history biographies | Originally published: London: Franklin Watts, 2019. | Includes index.
Identifiers: Canadiana (print) 20200359223 | Canadiana (ebook) 20200359231 | ISBN 9781427127938 (hardcover) | ISBN 9781427127990 (softcover) | ISBN 9781427128058 (HTML)
Subjects: LCSH: Winfrey, Oprah—Juvenile literature. | LCSH: Women television personalities—United States—Biography—Juvenile literature. | LCSH: African American television personalities—United States—Biography—Juvenile literature.
Classification: LCC PN1992.4.W56 H65 2021 | DDC j791.4502/8092—dc23

Library of Congress Cataloging-in-Publication Data

Names: Howell, Izzi, author.
Title: Oprah Winfrey / Izzi Howell.
Description: New York : Crabtree Publishing Company, 2021. | Series: Black history biographies | Includes index.
Identifiers: LCCN 2020045945 (print) | LCCN 2020045946 (ebook) | ISBN 9781427127938 (hardcover) | ISBN 9781427127990 (paperback) | ISBN 9781427128058 (ebook)
Subjects: LCSH: Winfrey, Oprah--Juvenile literature. | Women television personalities--United States--Biography--Juvenile literature. | African American television personalities--United States--Biography--Juvenile literature. | African American actresses--Biography--Juvenile literature. | African American women--Biography--Juvenile literature.
Classification: LCC PN1992.4.W56 H69 2021 (print) | LCC PN1992.4.W56 (ebook) | DDC 791.4502/8092 [B]--dc23
LC record available at https://lccn.loc.gov/2020045945
LC ebook record available at https://lccn.loc.gov/2020045946

Contents

Oprah Winfrey 4
Childhood 6
Reading the news 8
The Oprah Winfrey Show 10
Acting 12
Businesswoman 14
Helping others 16
Politics 18
Success 20
Quiz 22
Glossary 23
Index, answers, and teaching notes . . 24

Oprah Winfrey

Oprah Winfrey is an American television show host, **producer**, author, and actor.

◀ Oprah Winfrey goes to events to celebrate her new movies.

Can you name another TV show host or actor?

4

Oprah Winfrey is **famous** around the world. She uses her money and fame to try to make the world a better place.

Winfrey often gives speeches to people about things she thinks are important.

Childhood

Oprah Winfrey was born on January 29, 1954, in Kosciusko, Mississippi. She lived with her grandmother until she was six. Later, she lived with her mother in Milwaukee, Wisconsin.

▲ Oprah's grandmother was poor. They lived in a small house like this one.

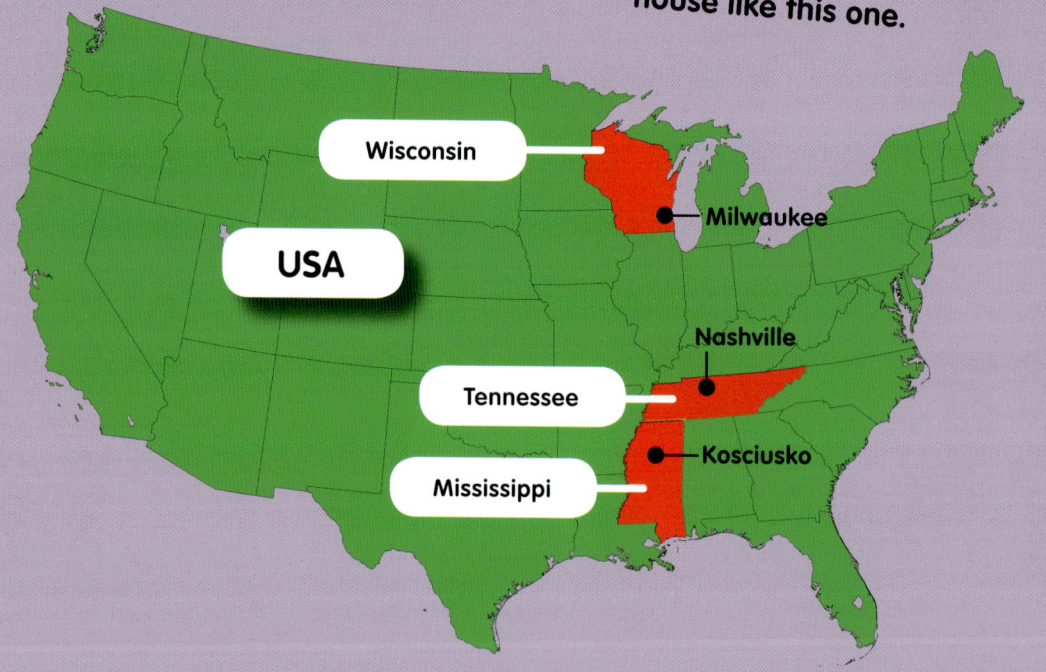

When she was 14, Oprah went to live with her father in Nashville, Tennessee. She did well at school. Drama was one of her favorite subjects.

Oprah won a competition when she was a teenager. ▼

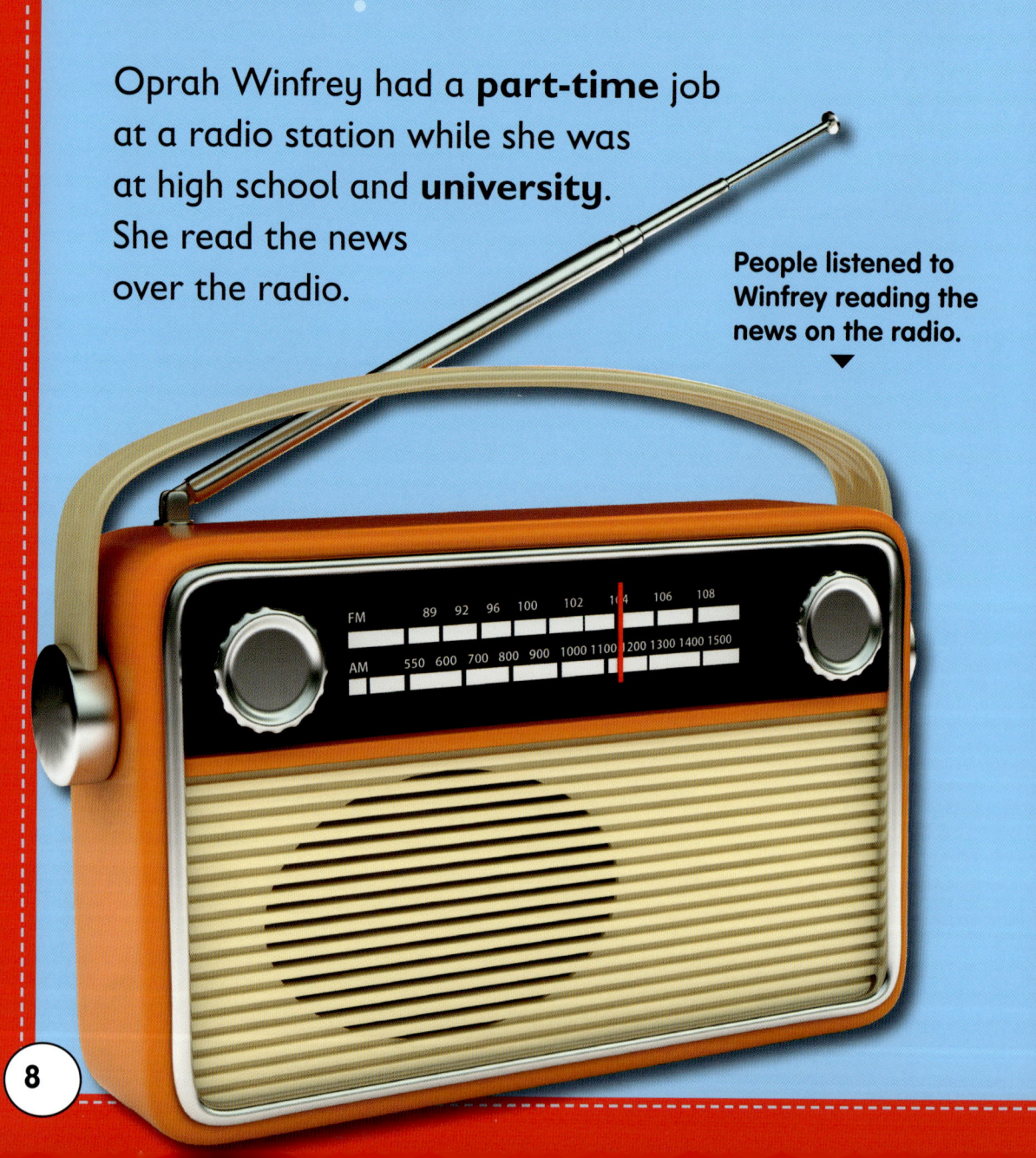

Reading the news

Oprah Winfrey had a **part-time** job at a radio station while she was at high school and **university**. She read the news over the radio.

People listened to Winfrey reading the news on the radio.

▲ Oprah Winfrey was a TV news host in the 1970s.

When Oprah Winfrey was 19, she left university to work at a TV station. She read the news on TV. She was the youngest person and the first Black woman to read the news on TV in Nashville.

How does your family learn about the news? Do you listen to the radio, watch TV, or another way?

The Oprah Winfrey Show

In 1984, Oprah Winfrey became the **host** of a talk show. The show became very popular. In 1986, the show was renamed *The Oprah Winfrey Show*.

People watched *The Oprah Winfrey Show* being filmed. Winfrey sometimes talked to them. ▼

On *The Oprah Winfrey Show*, Oprah Winfrey talked about different topics with special guests. Sometimes her guests were famous people. Others were people who had amazing or very difficult lives.

Winfrey interviewed Will Smith, a famous actor. ▶

Have you ever watched a talk show? Which one?

Acting

Oprah Winfrey has worked as an actor for many years. She has been in films and TV shows.

In 2018, Oprah Winfrey acted in the movie, *A Wrinkle in Time*. ▼

Have you ever seen a film starring Oprah Winfrey?

Oprah Winfrey is also a movie and TV producer. She chooses which show to make and organizes the actors and the **director**.

Oprah Winfrey has won many awards for her acting and producing. ▶

Businesswoman

Oprah Winfrey runs many successful businesses. She has her own magazine called *O – The Oprah magazine*.

▲ Oprah Winfrey is always on the front cover of her magazine.

She has also started businesses selling food and books. Her food business sells healthy food.

These mashed potatoes are made by Oprah's food business. ▶

▲ Oprah Winfrey has written different books about how to be happy.

Helping others

Oprah Winfrey often gives money to help other people. She gives money to schools, museums, and **charities**.

In 2002, Oprah met children from poor areas and gave them shoes and clothes. ▼

In 2007, Oprah Winfrey opened a school for girls in South Africa. The girls at the school come from poor families. The school helps them to get a good education.

Oprah Winfrey celebrated the opening of her school with the students. ▼

What do you do to help other people?

Politics

Oprah Winfrey is interested in **politics**. In 2008, she **campaigned** for Barack Obama to become the **president** of the United States. Many people **voted** for Obama because Oprah Winfrey supported him.

Oprah Winfrey helped Barack Obama to become the president of the U.S.A.

Michelle Obama (Barack Obama's wife)

Oprah Winfrey

Barack Obama

Oprah Winfrey still campaigns for different **politicians**. She wants America to be a fair and safe place to live.

▲ Some people think that Oprah Winfrey would be a good president.

Success

Oprah Winfrey's businesses have made her very **wealthy**. She is the wealthiest Black woman in the world.

◀ President Barack Obama gave Oprah Winfrey an important medal in 2013 to celebrate her successes.

Have you ever won a medal? What was it for?

Many people look up to Oprah Winfrey. She has worked very hard. She has taught people to be happy and love themselves.

Oprah Winfrey shares her life with her partner Stedman Graham. They have been together since 1986. ▼

Quiz

Test how much you remember.

Check your answers on page 24.

1. When was Oprah Winfrey born?

2. Which school subject did Oprah Winfrey like the best?

3. What was Oprah's part-time job during high school and university?

4. What was the name of Oprah Winfrey's talk show?

5. Name two of Oprah Winfrey's businesses.

6. Where is the school that Oprah Winfrey opened?

Glossary

awards Things given to someone to recognize their achievements

campaigned Organized and attended activities to try to achieve something

charities Companies or organizations that give money or help to people who need it

director Someone who tells actors what to do

famous Known by many people

host Someone who entertains guests or visitors

part-time Describes a job that only takes up part of your time

politicians People who work in government

politics Ideas about how a country is run by a government

president The leader of a country

producer Someone who controls how a film or TV show is made

speeches Talks that someone gives to groups of people

university A place where students study to get a degree

voted Showed your choice or opinion

wealthy Someone who has a lot of money or is rich

Index

acting 4, 11, 12–13

awards 13, 20

businesses 14, 15, 20

charities 16–17

childhood 6–7, 8

films 4, 12, 13

Graham, Stedman 21

magazines 14

money 5, 20

news 8–9

Obama, Barack 18, 20

politics 18–19

radio 8

schools 7, 8, 16, 17

The Oprah Winfrey Show 10–11

TV 4, 9, 12, 13

Answers:
1: January 29, 1954; 2: Drama; 3: Reading the news on the radio; 4: *The Oprah Winfrey Show*; 5: Making films and TV shows, her magazine, writing books, her food business; 6: South Africa

Teaching notes:
Some children should be able to enjoy this book as independent readers. Other children will need more support.

Before you share the book:
- What do readers already know about Oprah Winfrey?
- Introduce the idea of "celebrity." Explain that Oprah Winfrey is an American celebrity known throughout the world. Ask readers to think of other celebrities.

While you share the book:
- Help readers to read some of the more unfamiliar words.
- Talk about the questions. Encourage readers to make links between their own experiences and the events described.
- Discuss what you can learn about Oprah's life just by looking at the pictures in the book.

After you have shared the book, ask readers:
- Why do you think some people look up to Oprah Winfrey? Do you look up to her?
- Which success do you think she got her medal for?
- If you were a rich celebrity, how would you try to help people?